Growing Readers

New Hanover County Public Library

Purchased with
New Hanover County Partnership for Children
and Smart Start Funds

Let's Read About Food

# Fruit

by Cynthia Klingel and Robert B. Noyed
photographs by Gregg Andersen

Reading consultant: Cecilia Minden-Cupp, Ph.D.,
Adjunct Professor, College of Continuing and Professional Studies, University of Virginia

For a free color catalog describing
Weekly Reader® Early Learning Library's
list of high-quality books, call 1-800-542-2595
or fax your request to (414) 332-3567.

Library of Congress Cataloging-in-Publication Data available
upon request from publisher.  Fax (414) 336-0157 for the
attention of the Publishing Records Department.

ISBN 0-8368-3057-1 (lib. bdg.)
ISBN 0-8368-3146-2 (softcover)

This edition first published in 2002 by
**Weekly Reader® Early Learning Library**
330 West Olive Street, Suite 100
Milwaukee, WI  53212  USA

An Editorial Directions book
Editors: E. Russell Primm and Emily Dolbear
Art direction, design, and page production: The Design Lab
Photographer: Gregg Andersen
Weekly Reader® Early Learning Library art direction: Tammy Gruenewald
Weekly Reader® Early Learning Library production: Susan Ashley

Printed in the United States of America

1 2 3 4 5 6 7 8 9 06 05 04 03 02

# Note to Educators and Parents

As a Reading Specialist I know that books for young children should engage their interest, impart useful information, and motivate them to want to learn more.

*Let's Read About Food* is a new series of books designed to help children understand the value of good nutrition and eating to stay healthy.

A young child's active mind is engaged by the carefully chosen subjects. The imaginative text works to build young vocabularies. The short, repetitive sentences help children stay focused as they develop their own relationship with reading. The bright, colorful photographs of children enjoying good nutrition habits complement the text with their simplicity and both entertain and encourage young children to want to learn — and read — more.

These books are designed to be used by adults as "read-to" books to share with children to encourage early literacy in the home, school, and library. They are also suitable for more advanced young readers to enjoy on their own.

— Cecilia Minden-Cupp, Ph.D.,
Adjunct Professor, College of Continuing and
Professional Studies, University of Virginia

I like to eat fruit.
It is good for me.

We choose from six different kinds of food. We need to eat all six kinds every day to stay healthy.

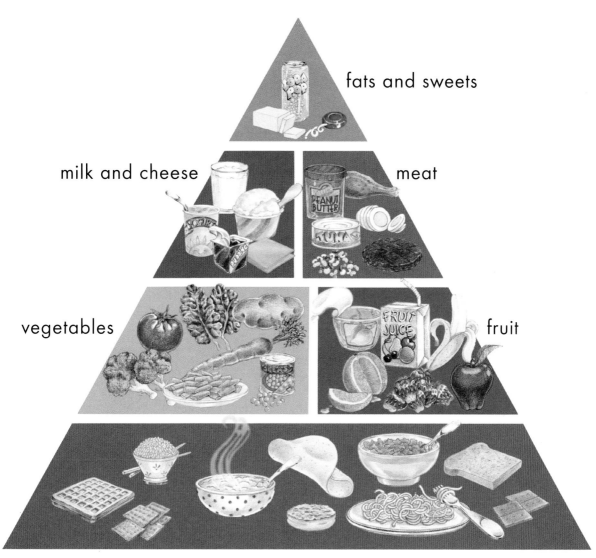

fats and sweets

milk and cheese

meat

vegetables

fruit

bread and cereal

My body gets vitamins from fruit. Oranges and strawberries have lots of vitamin C.

There are many kinds of fruit. I like apples in many different colors!

Some fruit is fuzzy.
Kiwis are fuzzy!

Some fruit is spiky. Pineapples are spiky!

Some fruit is small. Grapes, raspberries, and cranberries are small.

Some fruit is big. Watermelons, honeydew melons, and cantaloupes are big.

I am hungry for fruit. I will have a big fruit salad!

## Glossary

**healthy**—to be strong and free of illness

**spiky**—sharp and pointy

**vitamin**—one of the substances in food that is needed for good health

# For More Information

## Fiction Books

French, Vivian. *Oliver's Fruit*. New York: Orchard Books, 1998.

Rylant, Cynthia, and Arthur Howard. *Mr. Putter & Tabby Pick the Pears*. New York: Harcourt Brace, 1995.

Wallace, Nancy Elizabeth. *Apples, Apples, Apples*. Delray Beach, Fla.: Winslow Press, 2000.

## Nonfiction Books

Frost, Helen, and Gail Saunders-Smith. *The Fruit Group*. Mankato, Minn.: Pebble Books, 2000.

Kalman, Bobbie. *Hooray for Orchards!* New York: Crabtree Publications, 1997.

Royston, Angela. *Flowers, Fruits and Seeds*. Chicago: Heinemann Library, 1999.

## Web Sites

**Fruit ABC**

*www.thefruitpages.com/alphabet.shtml*

To see a fruit for every letter of the alphabet

# Index

## About the Authors

**Cynthia Klingel** has worked as a high school English teacher and an elementary school teacher. She is currently the curriculum director for a Minnesota school district. Cynthia Klingel lives with her family in Mankato, Minnesota.

**Robert B. Noyed** started his career as a newspaper reporter. Since then, he has worked in school communications and public relations at the state and national level. Robert B. Noyed lives with his family in Brooklyn Center, Minnesota.